HAL•LEONARD
INSTRUMENTAL
PLAY-ALONG

AUDIO
ACCESS
INCLUDED

PLAYBACK+
Speed • Pitch • Balance • Loop

ALTO SAX

STAR WARS

MUSIC FROM ALL NINE FILMS

Audio arrangements by Peter Deneff

To access audio, visit:
www.halleonard.com/mylibrary

"Enter Code"
6777-8981-6229-5434

ISBN 978-1-70510-711-9

HAL•LEONARD®

Visit Hal Leonard Online at
www.halleonard.com

Contact us:
Hal Leonard
7777 West Bluemound Road
Milwaukee, WI 53213
Email: info@halleonard.com

In Europe, contact:
Hal Leonard Europe Limited
42 Wigmore Street
Marylebone, London, W1U 2RN
Email: info@halleonardeurope.com

In Australia, contact:
Hal Leonard Australia Pty. Ltd.
4 Lentara Court
Cheltenham, Victoria, 3192 Australia
Email: info@halleonard.com.au

2

ACROSS THE STARS

(Love Theme from *"STAR WARS: ATTACK OF THE CLONES"*)

ALTO SAX

Music by JOHN WILLIAMS

AHCH-TO ISLAND

from *STAR WARS: THE LAST JEDI*

ALTO SAX

Music by JOHN WILLIAMS

BATTLE OF THE HEROES

from *STAR WARS: REVENGE OF THE SITH*

ALTO SAX

By JOHN WILLIAMS

CANTINA BAND

from *STAR WARS: A NEW HOPE*

ALTO SAX

Music by JOHN WILLIAMS

7

D.S. al Coda

CODA

DUEL OF THE FATES

from *STAR WARS: THE PHANTOM MENACE*

ALTO SAX

Music by JOHN WILLIAMS

THE FOREST BATTLE

from *STAR WARS: RETURN OF THE JEDI*

ALTO SAX

Music by JOHN WILLIAMS

HAN SOLO AND THE PRINCESS

from *STAR WARS: THE EMPIRE STRIKES BACK*

ALTO SAX

Music by JOHN WILLIAMS

THE IMPERIAL MARCH
(Darth Vader's Theme)
from *STAR WARS: THE EMPIRE STRIKES BACK*

ALTO SAX

Music by JOHN WILLIAMS

MARCH OF THE RESISTANCE

from *STAR WARS: THE FORCE AWAKENS*

ALTO SAX

Music by JOHN WILLIAMS

MAY THE FORCE BE WITH YOU

from *STAR WARS: A NEW HOPE*

ALTO SAX

Music by JOHN WILLIAMS

THE RISE OF SKYWALKER

from *STAR WARS: THE RISE OF SKYWALKER*

ALTO SAX

Composed by JOHN WILLIAMS

PRINCESS LEIA'S THEME

from *STAR WARS: A NEW HOPE*

ALTO SAX

Music by JOHN WILLIAMS

REY'S THEME

from *STAR WARS: THE FORCE AWAKENS*

ALTO SAX

Music by JOHN WILLIAMS

STAR WARS
(Main Theme)
from *STAR WARS: A NEW HOPE*

ALTO SAX

Music by JOHN WILLIAMS

THRONE ROOM *and* END TITLE

from *STAR WARS: A NEW HOPE*

ALTO SAX

Music by JOHN WILLIAMS

YODA'S THEME

from *STAR WARS: THE EMPIRE STRIKES BACK*

ALTO SAX

Music by JOHN WILLIAMS